All Else Is Bondage

Also by Wei Wu Wei

Open Secret

The Tenth Man

Posthumous Pieces

Unworldly Wise

All Else Is Bondage

Non-Volitional Living

WEI WU WEI

wisdom tree

Reprinted in India by arrangement with Sentient Publications.

Cover design by Kim Johansen, Black Dog Design
Book design by Anna Bergstrom and Nicholas Cummings

ISBN 978-81-8328-119-5

Published in 2008 by
Wisdom Tree
4779/23, Ansari Road, Darya Ganj
New Delhi-110 002
Ph.: 23247966/67/68

Printed at
Print Perfect
New Delhi-110 064

Deputy-Minister: But I am a profane man, I hold an Office, how could I study to obtain the Way?

Shen Hui: Very well, Your Honour, from to-day I will allow you to work on understanding only. Without practising, only reach understanding, then when you are deeply impregnated with your correct understanding, all the major entanglements and illusory thoughts gradually will subside. . . . In our school we indicate at once that it is the understanding which is essential without having recourse to a multitude of texts.

—SHEN HUI, h. 5

Yes, but then Shen Hui was there to promote the understanding: we only have him as one of a "multitude of texts."

Yes, he says it—understanding can suffice. But we must "live" that understanding—noumenally of course!

Contents

Foreword

All Else Is Bondage: Non-Volitional Living is the fourth of eight remarkable works by Wei Wu Wei that were originally published between 1958 and 1974. These works draw on a wide variety of sources including Taoism, especially the texts attributed to Lao Tzu and Chuang Tzu; Buddhism, most notably the Heart, Diamond, and Lankavatara Sutras; and Chan Buddhism as taught by Hui Neng, Huang Po, Hui Hai, and Shen Hui. The teachings of Padma Sambhava and Sri Ramana Maharshi, among others, are also frequently referred to.

What makes Wei Wu Wei's work remarkable is not only the breadth and unquestionable authenticity of these sources, but also the uncompromising nature of his interpretation of the truths expressed therein. In *All Else is Bondage* he examines one of the fundamental insights implicit in all these sources—this being that most of us live in a state of bondage and that this state is a direct consequence of our identification with an apparent object in relative reality. This identification—be it with the physical body or with the individualized ego—results in a lack of consciousness of our true nature. This true nature Wei Wu Wei characterizes as the underlying Subject, or "pure being," of which all apparent objects—our "selves" included—are simply a manifestation in the relative reality of space and time as perceived through the senses. In and of themselves, these apparent objects have no actual existence except as Subject Itself thus perceived. Simply put, we can either identify ourselves with one of these objects or be conscious of "ourselves" as the Subject underlying them all, the former being bondage and the latter being liberation. As Wei Wu Wei observes in this book,

> As long as we are identified with an object: that is bondage. As long as we think, act, live via an object, or as an object: that is bondage. As long as we feel ourselves to be an object, or think we are such (and a "self" is an object): that is bondage.
>
> —*All Else Is Bondage,* pp. 41

Once the nature of the problem is understood, the question that tends to arise is "How can one escape this condition?" Wei Wu Wei points out that at this stage there is the danger that the objectified self, or ego, may decide to make itself "more spiritual" in order to "attain" liberation and begin some sort of rigorous "spiritual practice" to achieve this end. But he sees this as merely a defensive measure on the part of the ego to sidestep the real issue—this being the fact of its own inexistence as an independent entity. In his first book, *Fingers Pointing Towards the Moon: Reflections of a Pilgrim on the Way* he notes that,

> There seem to be two kinds of searchers: those who seek to make their ego something other than it is, i.e. holy, happy, unselfish . . . and those who understand that all such attempts are just gesticulation and play-acting, that there is only one thing that can be done, which is to disidentify themselves with the ego, by realising its unreality, and by becoming aware of their eternal identity with pure Being. (pp. 118)

So the next question that arises is "How does one realise the unreality of the ego?" Wei Wu Wei points out that in order for this to occur we must fully comprehend, firstly on an intellectual level but then on a more intuitive level, not only the illusory nature of the ego, but also the illusory nature of relative reality itself, and much of this book is intended to help us come to such an understanding. Wei Wu Wei prods, nudges, and sometimes propels us in the right direction by exposing and undermining the most basic assumptions upon which our perception and conception of relative reality are based. He does this in part by challenging the way in which we experience this apparent "reality," especially the way in which we experience time and space. He also challenges our assumptions regarding individual volition within this "reality," especially the concept of free will, and then leads us towards the notion of "non-volitional living" referred to in the subtitle of this book. As Wei Wu Wei says,

> The purest doctrines, such as those of Ramana Maharshi, Padma Sambhava, Huang Po and Shen Hui, just teach that it is sufficient by analysis to comprehend that there is no entity which could have effective volition, that an apparent act of volition when in accord with the inevitable can only be a vain gesture and, when in discord, the fluttering of a caged bird against the bars of his cage. When he knows that, then at last he has peace and is glad.
>
> —*All Else is Bondage,* pp. 67-68

In short, what Wei Wu Wei does is help us to understand and experience our true nature by stripping away the various misconceptions that result in our identification with an illusory object or entity.

This may all sound a bit daunting, but as he says in his Preface to this work, "If it was easy, should we not all be Buddhas?" And this book is certainly not easy reading—it's both intellectually challenging and a hard-core, no-nonsense attack on the very roots of our bondage. But for those who feel Wei Wu Wei's words resonating with truths they already sense at some level, and who feel drawn to the challenges presented, this slim volume could prove to be of great value. It is unlikely, however, that the material found in this book will be fully grasped in a single reading even by those for whom the words resonate most strongly. But by dipping into this profound work from time to time they may well find themselves experiencing the occasional crucial insight—and eventually perhaps even coming to experience that extraordinary and truly indescribable liberation, from the perspective of which it is no doubt a simple, self-evident fact that, indeed, "all else is bondage."

MATT ERREY
Creator of the Wei Wu Wei Archives website
www.weiwuwei.8k.com
Bangkok, Thailand
March 2004

Preface

THERE SEEMS never to have been a time at which sentient beings have not escaped from the dungeon of individuality. In the East liberation was elaborated into a fine art, but it may be doubted whether more people made their escape from solitary confinement outside the organised religions than by means of them.

In the West reintegration was sporadic, but in recent years it has become a widespread preoccupation. Unfortunately its technical dependence on oriental literature—sometimes translated by scholars whose knowledge of the language was greater than their understanding of the subject—has proved a barrier which rendered full comprehension laborious and exceedingly long. Therefore it appears to be essential that such teaching as may be transmissible shall be given in a modern idiom and in accordance with our own processes of thought. But this presentation can never be given by the discursive method to which we are used for the acquisition of conceptual knowledge, for the understanding required is not conceptual and therefore is not knowledge.

This may account for the extraordinary popularity of such works as the *Tao Te Ching*, and in a lesser degree for that of the Diamond and Heart Sutras and Padma Sambhava's *Knowing the Mind.* For despite the accretion of superfluous verbiage in which the essential doctrine of some of the latter has become embedded, their direct pointing at the truth, instead of explaining it, goes straight to the heart of the matter and allows the mind itself to develop its own vision. An elaborately developed thesis must always defeat its own end where this subject matter is concerned, for only indication could produce this understanding, which requires an intuitional faculty, and it could never be acquired wholesale from without.

It may be doubted, however, whether an entirely modern presentation of oriental or perennial metaphysics would be followed or accepted as trustworthy at present. Probably an intermediate stage is necessary, during which the method should be a presentation in modern idiom supported by the authority of the great Masters, with whose thoughts and technical terms most interested people are at least generally familiar. Moreover the question is bedevilled by the use, which has become a convention, of terms, mostly of Sanskrit origin, the colloquial sense of which, accepted by the early translators, is still employed. Often this sense is considerably different from the technical meaning given these terms in the Chinese texts, and it occasionally implies almost exactly the opposite. These misleading terms are still used, which is a matter of no importance to those few who understand to what they refer, and for whom any word whatsoever would suffice, but are a serious hindrance to the pilgrim struggling to understand.

The inadequacy of the short paragraphs that follow is due to the insufficiency of their expression. They are offered in the hope that the verity which underlies them may penetrate the mist of their presentation and kindle a spark that shall develop into the flame of fulfillment.

Please be so good as to believe that there is nothing whatever mysterious about this matter. If it was easy, should we not all be Buddhas? No doubt, but the apparent difficulty is due to our conditioning. The apparent mystery, on the other hand, is just obnubilation, an inability to perceive the obvious owing to a conditioned reflex which causes us persistently to look in the wrong direction!

A Note on the Terms "Volition" and "Causation"

All phenomena, being the result of objectivisation, are necessarily conditioned and subjected to the chain of causation.

Causation, being subjected to what we conceive as Time and Space, implies Space-Time, and vice versa, so that causation and volition may be regarded as one.

Therefore every possible kind of temporal activity must be conditioned and subjected to the chain of causation.

Per contra whatever is intemporal, or whatever intemporality is, cannot be bound by the chain of causation—since it cannot be subjected to Space-Time.

But whatever we are, whatever sentient-beings may be, is intemporal, and that which appears in Space-Time is phenomenal only.

Volition, therefore, in its phenomenal aspect is a manifestation of an I-concept, and it must be an element in the chain of causation, whereas "volition" in its noumenal aspect is not in fact such at all, is never manifest as such, and functions as an unidentifiable urge, as spontaneity, independent of deliberation, conceptualisation, and all phenomenal activity.

This noumenal volition is neither volition nor non-volition: it is volition that is non-volition, as *wei* is the action that is *wu wei*, for all interference on the part of an I-concept is excluded, and action (*wei*) is the expression of volition.

Ultimately it is what intemporally we are, for it is devoid of objectivity. It is what all sentient beings are, all Nature that comes into manifestation and returns to non-manifestation, that is born or sprouts, grows, matures, reproduces and dies. It is the non-volitional living which is that of a Man of Tao.

Noumenally

Who is there to possess or exercise volition? Who is there to experience the results of volition?

Who is there to create a cause? Who is there to suffer an effect?

There is no entity to exercise volition, there is no entity to suffer the results of volition.

There is neither a causal nor an effectual entity.

Phenomenally

Phenomenal subject-object are themselves results of temporality.

Phenomenal cause-effect are themselves dependent on the apparent seriality of time.

Phenomenal subject-object are never apart, are not independent entities: they are one whole concept revealing the mechanism of manifestation.

Phenomenal cause-effect are never separate, each is both, dependent on time, describing the temporal operation of the manifested universe.

Phenomenal subject-object and cause-effect not only are each a single concept divided by the temporal illusion, both are aspects of a single concept and are identical.

Therefore they can be called "causal subject-effectual object," and causation is a name for the process of objectivisation whereby the sensorial universe is produced.

I repeat: only an object can suffer, for it requires an object to experience suffering, and only an object can suffer the effect of a cause.

Therefore only objects can be involved in causation and conditioning, for phenomenal subject becomes object at the instant of any such occurrence.

Noumenal subjectivity must be eternally unaffected by causation. Noumenal subjectivity is eternally unconditioned and unbound.

Zero – Enlightenment and the Extinction of "Me"

DOING AWAY with the I-notion is the same as not desiring the personal attainment of enlightenment.

Not desiring that (the "last desire," the "last barrier") is "having it," for "having it" is in any case merely being rid of that which concealed what is forever that which alone we are.

Therefore not desiring personal attainment of that is at the same time the elimination of the I-notion which constitutes its concealment.

The *idea* of liberation automatically inhibits the simple realisation that we are free.

Note: Free, we are not number One, the first of all our objects, but *Zero*—their universal and Absolute Subject. This is illustrated by the famous "TENTH MAN" story.

1 · Thought

THE MASTERS' exhortations to abjure "thinking" do not imply the suppression of thought but the reorientation, by articulation, of the impetus that results in dualistic thought into its im-mediate experience.

Suppressed thought is the negative aspect of the dualism "thought-no-thought," another mode of thought itself and "one half of a pair," whereas what the Masters mean is *wu nien*, which is the absence of both counterparts, thought and no-thought, which is the presence of the suchness of thought, and that is expressed in spontaneous Action (pure action arising from Non-action: *Wu wei*).

WU NIEN is the presence of the absence of no-thought.

2 ·- *Truth*

THE SEEING of Truth cannot be dualistic (a "thing" seen).

It cannot be seen by a see-er, or via a see-er.

There can only be a seeing which itself is Truth.

The unfree (those still bound by objectivisation) want an object to be relative reality (relatively existing), i.e. that it should be projected independently of the see-er of it. This is basically dualistic.

But an object is projected via the see-er of it, and the seeing of it is at the same time its projection.

The unfree want two independent processes:

i. The Functioning of Principal localised as an object,

ii. The object perceived by a sentient being, himself an object projected by Principal.

But

i. The sentient being is himself Subject and Object, i.e. Principal in so far as he IS, as projected object generally interpreted as "John Smith" in so far as he is an object of perception.

ii. The generalised interpretation of the projection of Principal as "John Smith" is an object, an appearance only: that which he IS is Principal Whose apparent Functioning subjects him to such generalised interpretation on the part of "other" generalised aspects of that Functioning that are such as apparently independent objects in space-time.

The unfree wish a projected object, "John Smith" to perceive another projected object that is independently existing, but "John Smith," as a projected object, cannot see anything, being himself only a percept. In so far as he can be said to perceive, it is as the Functioning of Principal (that which he

IS) that he perceives, and the Function of perceiving by Principal is itself projection ("creation").

Note: "Projected" here is intended to cover the total process of interpretation whereby a percept becomes a phenomenal object sensorially perceived and conceptualised as such.

3 · Inconceivable

THE SPACE-TIME, subject-object phenomenal universe is a manifestation of mind, of which day and sleep dreaming are examples in a second degree.

The result of this individualisation process, based on seriality, which all degrees of dreamers know as "reality," has no objective resemblance to that which causes it to appear, because that which causes it to appear has no objective quality at all.

Therefore that is totally inaccessible to any form of objective cognition, let alone of description. The only words that can indicate it at all are This, Here, Now, and Am, and in a context which is entirely abstract.

The negative method is provisional only; it turns from the positive to its counterpart, and then negates both. That wipes out everything objective and leaves an emptiness which represents fullness, total absence which represents total presence. Here the thinking (and not-thinking) process ends, and the absence itself of that IS the Inconceivable.

Inconceivable for whoever attempts to conceive it. But who suggested that we should do that?

4 ~ It: On Realising Mind

When Time stops the universe disappears

It is here all the time precisely because it is beyond the reach of time; and it cannot be held because time is intermittent.

It is present in every now-moment between the tic-toc of serial manifestation via which it functions indirectly.

We know it eternally. It is the background not only of thought—as Maharshi told us—but of every act of living.

That is why it is pure Function, and what pure Function is.

> *It is too clear* and so it is hard to see.
> A dunce once searched for a fire with a lighted lantern.
> *Had he known what fire was,*
> He could have cooked his rice much sooner.
>
> —MUMON

It is the function whose dualistic and temporal manifestation is living, the act of every action, the origin of every thought, the basis of every percept, not directly what we do, what we think, what we see, subject to Time, what we project serially in the sensing as each phenomenal object. It is the living itself of life, not the way we live it objectively.

The awakened can live directly (as the "Zen" archer or swordsman can act directly), "we" live indirectly, but even indirect living is ultimately it—for it, not the "wooden puppet," the object, is all that we ARE.

"The mind or the mouth cannot act of their own accord," said Maharshi, "Recognise the force of the Divine Will and keep quiet!" And again:

"The mind or the mouth cannot act without the Self."

5 ⁓ Gone with My Head

MY HEAD is the centre of the universe.

Everything I see, sense, know is centred in my head (and in yours, and in the beetle's).

All are objects in which my head is subject (mediate Subject as a head, ultimate subject as "I").

But I cannot see, sense, or know my head, and the inference of its existence is inadmissible, sensorially unjustifiable. I perceive no such object, all other objects but not that. My head alone is not my object.

Of course not: it is subject, and an eye cannot see itself, I cannot sensorially perceive myself, subject cannot know itself—for that which is known is thereby an object. Subject cannot subsist as its own object.

So, all that is object *appears* to exist;

Subject alone does not *appear* to exist.

But object cannot exist apart from subject, whose manifest aspect it is.

Therefore it is *apparently* inexistent subject that IS, and *apparently* existent object that IS not.

Yet, since object is subject, and subject is object, intemporally that which they are, all that they can be, and all that IS, is the absence of my head (and of yours, and of the beetle's), which is also the presence of everything.

Where, then, am I? Where, then, are you, and the beetle?

We are our absence.

With apologies to Mr. Douglas Harding, whose On Having No Head *should not be held responsible, and which says so much more so much better.*

6 · *This Phenomenal Absence*

NOWHERE, WHERE I am an object, am I; nor where any part of "me" is an object is it part of me or is mine. Only here where I can see nothing (but the objective universe) am I—and I am only an absence objectively.

When I realise that, I cease also to be an individual "I," *for anything individual* is thereby an object.

My objective absence is the presence of pure non-objectivity, which is just that.

My only existence is non objective, as non-objectivity itself.

I cannot be portrayed in any way, drawn, photographed or described. That which impersonally I am has no qualities or resemblance to an individual subject-object, which is purely conceptual.

Note: A "self," an "ego," any kind of separated personality or being, is an object. That is why nothing of the kind is—as the Diamond Sutra so repeatedly insists.

My objective self only has a conceptual existence.

Non-objectively I am the apparent universe.

Identifying myself with my conceptual object is what constitutes bondage. Realising that my conceptual object only exists in so far as it and its subject are THIS phenomenal absence here and now—constitutes liberation.

I am my phenomenal absence.

7 · *Our Buddha-Nature*

THERE IS no mystery whatever—only the inability to perceive the obvious.

"He has nowhere to hide!" as Mumon put it.

The supposed or apparent "mystery" is due to the objective inexistence of pure non-objectivity—which is the Buddha-nature, because objectivity is only conceptual, and non-objectivity is incompatible with any degree of positivity.

Huang Po said it categorically, "Our original Buddha-nature is, in highest truth, devoid of any atom of objectivity."

What is there mysterious in This-here-now-am, which is everywhere, and apart from which nothing else is?

This which IS is pure presence, autonomous and spontaneous.

It is This which is looking for Itself when we look for It, and we cannot find It because It is This which we are.

Objectively *It is not here.*

Note: Dualistic language does not permit us to express these things without the use of objective terms such as "it." There is no such word as "thisself," nor can the word "this" be repeated indefinitely, and it is only a pointer in any case. The *sense* must maintain an uninterrupted subjectivity.

8 · This Which We Are

SINCE WE are obliged to use dualistic language in order to communicate understanding we should be well-advised to use words in a manner which is verifiable, that is in a way which is etymologically correct.

To per-ceive means "thoroughly to take hold of," but metaphysically there is no one to take hold of anything and nothing to take hold of. Therefore perception is the first stage cf the conceptualisation process, and the two elements—perception and conception—form one whole, and that one whole is the mechanism whereby we create *samsara.*

What we are required to do is the contrary, to lay everything down, to be nothing, to know that we are nothing, and thereby leave behind the whole process of conceptualisation. So-doing we cease to be that which we never were, are not, and never could be. That, no doubt, is *nirvana*, and, since nothing is being conceived, nothing is being perceived, and nothing is being "projected" via the psycho-somatic apparatus which itself is a conceptualised percept.

At that moment the phenomenal universe no longer exists as far as we are concerned. We are "sitting in a *bodhimandala*," in a state of perfect availability. So placed—and automatically—we should re-become integrally that which we always were, are, and forever must be. And that—because it is THIS—can never be thought or spoken, for this, being purely non-objective, is in a different "direction of measurement" from any conceptual dimension, being the source of all dimensionality and phenomenality.

THIS is the sun itself, shining through the dualism of negative and positive, whose rays (which are Itself) appear to split into that negative (*nirvana*) and that positive (*samsara*) from which arise all phenomena, the perceptual-conceptual universe, including that which we have known as ourselves.

"I am that I am," said Jahweh—which no doubt means "this which I am." We, too are "this which we are," for THIS is everything that ever was, is, or could be.

9 · *Potential Reality*

THE EXTROVERT assumes that things objectively exist, and that subjectively they do not. That indeed is the accepted sense of those terms and, I think, the theoretical and experimental basis of science.

It requires years of intuitive research to understand that the opposite is the truth, that no thing exists objectively other than as a concept, and that subjectively every thing has potential existence, i.e. permanently exists as potential.

When the Masters say tirelessly that every single thing "neither exists nor does not exist" they mean just that: its only existence is as potential which is the integration of object and subject, of negative and positive, by which each interdependent counterpart has been obliterated.

The term "realisation"—"making real, a thing"—logically is only applicable to the illusory process of assuming conceptual objects do exist, for *they have no other* reality.

That which ultimately they ARE, and all that they could ever BE, is neither Reality nor Relative Reality (even with capital "R"s) but Potential (with a capital "P" if you wish).

10 ·– Potential Plenum

THE MASTERS' constant formula, in a sense their essential "teaching," taking any and every *dharma* and declaring that it "neither is nor is not," means precisely (and factually) that it "is neither positive nor negative." Therefore it is idle to do what we are apt to do, that is immediately to look for that which it ("really," as we say) is—since we are begging the question, having just been told that *it* IS not.

That which is not positive and not negative is the result of the mutual extinction, or negation, of each (Shen Hui's double negative), by means of which each characteristic is cancelled by its counterpart (as light by shade, and shade by light, in positive and negative films), leaving a phenomenal blank, no phenomena whatever, that is perfect objective voidness, unhappily, even absurdly, called "*The* Void."

Shen Hui has stated that, to the awakened, voidness no longer is such–which means that voidness no longer appears as an object. But that which, viewed objectively, is void can never *be* anything else, can never, for instance, be "full," a "plenum," as has been maintained (but never, I think, by a Master): that whose identity is voidness of objects can never not be void of objects without ceasing to be what it is. As long as it is itself an object, it must remain devoid of objects, but when it ceases to be an object, ceases to be itself at all, it thereby returns to subject, as which it is pure potential, and, as such, a *potential plenum.*

That, no doubt, is the sense of Shen Hui's statement, which has caused some disturbance in the heads of the scholars.

Note: May we not generalise from this and declare that the same applies to all objects? Is it not evident that every object, when it ceases to be itself, i.e. objective, thereby becomes void, returns to subject and re-becomes potentiality–which is all that anything IS? Always bearing in mind that "potentiality" is only a pointing, not any "thing," for phenomenally it must ever be total absence, which non-objectively must be total presence, just as what objectively is void, subjectively is a plenum.

11 · Potential Being

RETURNING OBJECT to subject—called "Returning Function to Principal" in some translations of the Ch'an Masters—should be returning "it" (whatever it be) to potentiality. On the other hand the projection of phenomena, the sensorially-perceived universe, or objectivisation, may be said to occur via the dualistic mechanism of temporality, that is by splitting of potentiality, which is unitary, into subject and object, which then becomes a pseudo-subject "perceiving" as negative and positive, and an intellectual interpretation of that as the projected image which is accepted as really existing.

Thus "perceiving" itself is seen as a dual process in Time, an in-formal giving-out, taken-in as form, and then objectively interpreted. The in-formal giving-out, sometimes called "pure perception," may perhaps be regarded as *bodhi*, whereas the taking-in, or normal perception and its intellectual interpretation are psycho-somatic and illusory.

The "identity" of Form and Void in the sutras is an expression of this dual aspect of "perceiving"—"in-formal" articulated into "form" by the mechanism of the *skandhas* and interpreted by the cognising sixth sense.

But to understand this objectively has little practical value. It must happen to us. It is happening to "us" incessantly. It is that by which "we" are being "lived." If, instead of letting it "live" "us," we live it—we find we are it and it is all that we are.

12 ~ Enfin

PERHAPS WE have said too often that objects do not exist, perhaps we have repeated—so often that it has become an empty formula—that there is no self; and, perhaps, it may not even be quite true? Indeed nothing expressed by split-mind could ever be anything whole.

After all, do we not know that every *dharma* (thing, object) neither exists nor does not exist?

May we not have stopped half-way, failed to penetrate to the heart of the matter, remained only half-turned away from the wrong direction of looking? We may have lacked the insight to insee the living truth.

If a monk had said to a T'ang Master what we have been saying, with the same assured self-satisfaction that we have said it, would he not have received thirty blows with the magisterial staff instead of the acquiescence he smugly anticipated? If so, what would he have said if, as a result of his beating, he had been happy enough to see the whole truth in a flash of pure insight?

Would he not have said "Objects are not *objects* at all, no 'object' is an *object*"?

The phrase "an object is not an object" is not the same as the phrase "no object exists." Why so? It may mean that an object is something else. Non-existence is a mode of existence, existence and non-existence are a pair of interdependent counterparts, neither of which can exist alone, as "half of a pair," as Huang Po told us: they must find their resolution in their mutual negation.

Let us take an example, the classic one. We have said that an ego does not exist, is not at all, at all. But in fact it neither exists nor non-exists, so what? "*Ego is not an ego at all*"—that is surely the inseeing of the matter? And what does that mean? It means the "ego" is never an object. It does not state that it cannot be something else. But what could it be, what could anything be, that is not an object?

All we can say is that the nearest we can get to indicating anything that is not an object—for even subject becomes an object for us when it is objectified as such in thought or its verbal expression—is to refer to it as non-object.

So, since objects are *not* objects at all they might perhaps be considered as non-objects, and "an ego" (or "a self") as being non-ego (or no-self). But what is non-object or non-ego (or no-self)?

II. The Corral

What is it? Is it not the object, ego, self, when that is not an object, ego, self? Is that not why the Masters of Ch'an as of Vedanta, that is of all *Advaita*, occasionally shake us up by remarking that phenomena are real, that even concepts are real? After all, nothing is either more or less real than anything else—for reality too (being a concept, an object), is not at all "real" (since it is objective), and can only be such in its negation.

Then all that is left to us to ask is what is anything, what are all things, "material" or "psychic," when they are not THAT, when they are "devoid of all trace of objectivity" (Huang Po)? Obviously since they are not any thing objective at all we could not, in the seriality of time, find a name for what they are, for whatever name we found would make them that which they are not. So an answer as such, can only be negative from our dualistic standpoint.

Colloquially might we not say that it is misleading to *think* that "all things are nothing," but revelatory to *perceive* that "every thing is no-thing, i.e. not a *thing*"? Why? Because this non-conceptual non-objectivity which they, all things, ARE—is THIS, not that.

How obvious the answer is! But how frustrating!—since we cannot think it, much less give it a name, make a word of it, without thereby turning it back into the object which it is not!

But does that matter? Does it not suffice to insee it? Does not that inseeing itself destroy all need, together with all possibility, of conceptualising it? And that just because the inseeing is the answer? The eye which cannot see itself knows neither need nor regret for the non-eye that it is.

Note: Let us be careful not to draw conclusions that the premises do not warrant. Let us remember that "that which is perceived cannot perceive," as Huang Po told us. The perceived is the "object" which, as such, cannot perceive—only this which it is—non-object—can do that. And that because object is subject and subject is object.

In short: the sensorially-perceived universe is *not at all* objective.

And THIS is not the see-er of that, but the looking at it.

It is thought and no-thought, mind and no-mind, action and non-action, self and no-self, object and no-object, as concepts, each one and all regarded conceptually, that *are not* as such, and their so-called suchness, isness, quiddity is the presence of their phenomenal and conceptual, absence.

13 ~ *Seeking the Seeker*

THAT WHICH you seek and cannot find—is the Seeker.

The reason why the "Dharmakaya" cannot be found or described is that ultimately IT is the Seeker, the Describer, which is seeking—and so would be *the Subject making an object of Itself.*

Every time you try to name THIS-HERE-NOW you are an eye trying to see itself. You cannot objectify THIS-WHICH-YOU-ARE, and that which you can objectify is THAT-WHICH-YOU-ARE-NOT.

> THIS which is seeking is THAT which is sought, and
> THAT which is sought is THIS which is seeking.

"Dharmakaya" is just Mind (which cannot be found because, sought, it is the Seeker); and "Shunyata" (void) is what an eye does not see when it tries to look at itself.

But there is no "Dharmakaya," no "Mind," no "Shunyata"—no thing whatever to be sought. And there is no "thing" whatever to seek any other "thing."

Nor is there anyone to experience their total absence which is also his own.

When Bodhidharma told Hui K'o to bring him his mind so that he might tranquillise it, and Hui K'o failed to find it, Bodhidharma said "There you see—I have tranquillised it for you," what then enlightened Hui K'o? He saw that the sought was the Seeker, and that the seeker was the Sought.

When Huang Po said "You cannot use Mind to seek Mind, the Buddha to seek the Buddha, or the Dharma to seek the Dharma," he pointed at the same essential truth. The sought cannot seek, for the sought can only be the seeker.

Padma Sambhava, the supreme Master, said "There are no two such things as sought and seeker (also practice and practiser, thought and thinker, action and actor); when fully comprehended, the sought (practice, etc.) is found to be one with the seeker (practiser, etc.). If the seeker himself, when sought, cannot be found, thereupon is attained the goal of the seeking (practising, etc.) and also the end of the search itself. Then nothing more is there to be sought, nor is there any need to seek anything." He adds "Inasmuch as from eternity there is nothing whatsoever to be practised, there is no need to fall under the sway of erroneous methods."

Here again, and in all these statements, this understanding is the understanding of all that is to be understood, of all that need be understood, perhaps of all that can be understood—for is anything else fundamentally and entirely true? Here again the integral understanding of this is itself the Awakened state.

And the only practice is seeing this, which is Awareness, which is this which an eye cannot see when it looks at itself.

Practice is deepening understanding, for understanding is first an intuitional glimpse of the truth of this, then the obtaining of this intuitional glimpse at will, and, finally, the permanent installation of this inseeing when "walking, standing, sitting and lying," in public and in private, asleep and awake.

14 ~ Pure Function

THIS WHICH seeks is That which is sought; That which is sought is This which seeks.

There is no seeker, and no thing sought.

The *functioning* of "seeking" in whole-mind is conceptualized by split-mind as Seeker and Sought.

This which objectivises is That which is objectivised; That which is objectivised is This which objectivises.

There is no objectiviser, there is no thing objectivised.

Objective *functioning* of whole-mind is conceptualized by split-mind as Subject and Object.

This which acts is That which is done; That which is done is This which acts.

There is no do-er, and no thing done.

The *functioning* of whole-mind is conceptualized by split-mind as Actor and Action.

This which thinks is That which is thought; That which is thought is This which thinks.

There is no thinker, and there is no object of thought

The *functioning* of "thinking" by whole-mind is conceptualized by split-mind as Thinker and Thought.

This which practices is That which is practiced; that which is practiced is This which practices.

There is no practicer, and no thing is practiced.

The *functioning* of practicing by whole-mind is conceptualized by split-mind as Practicer and Practice.

Note: The only possible justification for the term "the Mean," which, in any other connotation is metaphysically nonsense, is in this context: "seek*ing*," "objectivis*ing*," "act*ing*," "think*ing*," "practic*ing*"—i.e., pure function. It represents the "mean" between "seeker and sought," "practicer and practice," etc., etc., and thereby may suggest pure function.

"Pure" function means function which is "chemically" uncontaminated by any kind of "object" whatsoever, i.e., spontaneous and unconditioned function*ing* of Principal, or just Immediacy.

15 ·⌣ Ultimate

From the beginning not a thing is.

—HUI NENG

This which I am is That (which I am not),
That which I am not is This (which I am).
There is neither This nor That.
I neither am nor am not (there is neither an I which is nor an I which is not).
There is neither whole-mind nor split-mind.
There is nothing to function, and no functioning.
There is no absence and no presence.
There still remains spontaneous immediacy?
It, also, neither is nor is not.
Now do you understand that there is not a thing to be understood?
WHO has understood, What has not understood?
WHO has been lived all these years, What has suffered?
Requiescat in pace; de mortuis. . . .

16 ⁓ "Once More unto the Breach, Dear Friends. . . ."

THERE IS no objective ego or self. Nothing of the kind could be as an object. Even the words themselves do not admit of it.

Did the Buddha mean anything but that in his insistence on the non-existence of a "self" of any kind whatsoever?

I am—but not, not ever, not possibly—as an object.

Our state of apparent bondage is due to identification with an imaginary objectivisation of "I." I became identified with my selves, and my selves are all sentient beings. Whenever we think or speak as from the object with which we are illusorily identified we are *thereby making an object of subject.*

That is why disidentification, or awakening from the objective dream of living, cannot take place as a result of thinking or of speaking.

What, then, am I since I can never be an object? Evidently THIS could never be thought, let alone named, without thereby making me THAT which I am not.

Perhaps one could say: "I am, but there is no 'me'," or "You are pure I: there is no 'you'." For indeed *there is no "I"*—but I am.

Do not nearly all of us spend our time looking for ourself as some object other than ourself—as Reality, "the" Absolute, God, Tao, Pure Mind? Is that not the quintessence of nonsense? The idea of "an I" or of "a self" is absurd, manifestly absurd, even linguistically. No "I" is. But I am.

If that is clear, then we must be able to see that THAT which we are looking for is not THAT but THIS—and THIS is "I am." There is no That and no This, no self and no other, no man and no God, no Buddha, Tao, Absolute, no Reality and no Unreality, no "you" or "me." I am no object, you are pure I. And I am utterly absent.

We have completed the circle: the Sought is the Seeker—and *there is none.* All else is just bondage.

17 ⁓ Genesis

I move,
Space becomes (as a result of my movement),
Time is born (as a measure of my movement in space),
I have objects (because I have become the subject of space and time),
Dualism is established, The Universe appears,
I identify myself with my objects (and there are illusory egos),
I suffer illusorily (and suffering becomes universal).

II. Metanoesis

I repose,
Space vanishes (for I have ceased to move),
Time ceases (for there is no movement to measure),
There are no objects (for I am no longer a subject),
Dualism is no more,
The universe disappears,
There are no illusory egos,
There is no suffering,
I am, but there is no "me."

18 – ?

WHAT AM I?

As far as I can understand I am the absence of my presence and the absence of the presence of my absence.

What does that mean?

It means that I am my phenomenal absence, and also the absence of that still phenomenal absence itself.

The resulting absence is phenomenally total, but it is not noumenally nil—or what is sometimes called pure nihilism.

It is an absence of all possible phenomenal presence which is itself, noumenally, whatever I am.

That is entirely no thing, for which reason it can neither be named nor described, which means that it is neither the "that" nor the "it" by which terms I have just referred to it.

But the establishment of "its" total phenomenal inexistence as an object of sense, or of thought, as a thing in itself, in no way implies its intemporal nullity.

On the contrary, the very temporal inexistence of itself as an object of consciousness, requires and indicates intemporal Isness.

19 ·- *Aeternitas*

The Non-Conceptual Universe

The phenomenal universe is essentially temporal—time being the measure of movement in space. By "essentially" I mean that its phenomenality is due entirely to its space-time conditioning, that is to the facts that it is extended in space and serialised in duration. As such, and as perceived as an object of subject, it is what science recognises as real despite its impermanence and phenomenality. Reality is "thingness," realisation is "recognising something as a thing" or reification, and there is no reality or realisation that is other than phenomenal. Such is temporality.

Intemporality is not basically different; it is not something else. It is that same temporal universe deprived of extension in space and of seriality in time, and as such it cannot be perceived as having form or attributes; and it necessarily appears as voidness. Intemporally the intemporal universe cannot in fact be perceived at all, except as Awareness, because it is no longer a thing, an object. Therefore it is no longer "real."

In the foregoing the term "real" is correctly used, for reality and unreality are concepts as phenomenal and objective as the perceptible universe itself, and they cannot correctly be applied to the noumenal and non-objective, which is neither real nor unreal and cannot be conceived as any "thing" or as possessing any attribute which, as such, is necessarily objective.

It follows that, unlike the temporal universe, the intemporal universe cannot be perceived as an object of subject. The reason of that should be quite obvious: it is not the object of any subject. It is subject, and an eye cannot see itself. And subject is not as such—for, as such, even subject becomes an object, a concept. If it must be referred to, it may be convenient to indicate it as being Eternity.

Every sentient being may say "This-which-I-am is not a concept," for bodhisattva or beetle has no self—but there is no thing in the temporal universe which is not his self in intemporality. Intemporality, or the intemporal universe, is the potentiality of which the temporal universe is the actuality, the unmanifested of which the temporal is the manifested, the subjectivity of which the temporal is the objectivisation.

But they are not two. There is only one universe—and it is This-which-we-are.

II

This *Aeternitas,* or intemporality, which is all that the bodhisattva is, all that the beetle is, all that every sentient being is, both phenomenally and noumenally, has no objective existence whatever. That is why it "neither exists nor does not exist"—which means that it is purely conceptual as an object.

That is why neither bodhisattva nor beetle has a self.

The second Patriarch, Hui K'o, having been asked by Bodhidharma to bring him his mind so that he might tranquillise it, replied that he had searched for it all night and had not been able to find it. The bodhisattva and the beetle may do likewise, may search for their self, not only all through a night but all through the years, and never will they find the slightest trace of a self. The reason for that is the same as the reason for Hui K'o's failure, and the result will be the same—awakening to the truth. Provided that the bodhisattva, or the beetle, understands what Hui K'o understood, which is that the conceptual object for which he was seeking is itself, from eternity, the seeker of that object.

But just as he could not find the object sought, so he was unable to find the seeker of that object—for, in looking for the seeker, he was making an object of it and, again, that which he sought was the seeker—for the seeker was the sought.

That is the sense in which there is no self, could never be a self, for "I" could never be an object, or a concept which would automatically make it such. The bodhisattva and the beetle ARE, but not as bodhisattva and beetle: all sentient beings ARE, but not as sentient beings.

What then are we? We are no things: we are, but there is no us. Intemporally we are unmanifest, the source of phenomenality: temporally all phenomena appear to exist and so are our self.

III. Description of No-Time

Intemporally there is no present, for the future becomes the past before the temporal process of perception and interpretation can be completed. The "present" is a theoretical line of demarcation like the equator.

Intemporally there is no past, as Huang Po stated, simply because there is no objective event to pass, and no *where* for any event as such to pass to.

Intemporally there is no future, as Huang Po stated also, simply because there is no objective event to become such, and no *where* for any event as such to come from.

After all, does it seem very difficult to see? After all, does it not even seem just a little odd—or "wondrous" as Padma Sambhava would have put it—that such a notion as serial time, composed of a purely theoretical past, present and future, should ever have become a current belief?

Description of No-Space

In-formally there can be no space because there is no objective entity as such to be extended therein, and conceptualised percepts can only extend conceptually.

In-formally there is no movement because there is no objective thing as such to move, and therefore no time is required to measure its movement, movement and time being purely conceptual.

In-formally there is no shape or colour, size, dimension or separation because these are all conceptual interpretations of percepts, and percepts have no objective validity, their validity being entirely non-objective and, therefore, as such informal.

Believing the Buddha

There is no existence, no being, that is other than conceptual. There is no existence or being that is not phenomenal.

There are no such states as existence and being. They are only cognisable as phenomenal experiences—which are concepts in temporality.

All things appear to be, conceptually, as objects in the temporal universe; no things appear to be in the intemporal universe, wherein they are not at all as things.

All things are potentially in the intemporal universe, for herein there is only pure unconditioned subjectivity, and that is not cognisable as such. It cannot be experienced at all, for even pure unconditioned self-awareness is not aware of awareness.

If you believe the Buddha, or if you see it for yourself—in either case it must necessarily be so.

20 · All Else Is Bondage

IF SUBJECT were red, there could be no red; if Subject were blue, there could be no blue.

If Subject were a pot, a mountain, any form, shape, sound, taste or odour, these could not be known.

If Subject were any object, material or conceptual, there could not be any object, material or conceptual.

Why? Because if Subject were an object it could not be the subject of that, or of any object.

Subject, then, must be transparent in order that opaqueness may appear,

Subject must be no thing in order that any thing may seem to exist,

Subject must be noumenon (apperception) in order that phenomena may be perceptible.

Subject must be Absence in order that there may be phenomenal Presence.

Subject is the sense of all the big words that seek to suggest the Ultimate—the Absolute, Tao, Reality, One Mind, the Essence of Mind, Pure Consciousness, the Dharmakaya, Atma, Brahman, the One, etc. etc.; and the other big words indicate aspects and function of Subject—Sat, Chit, Ananda, Prajna, Karuna, Bodhi, etc. They all point only at Subject—subject which can never be an object.

But since no object exists as a thing-in-itself it only appears to exist as an object of Subject.

As such it cannot be any thing: it is nothing but Subject, and, phenomenally, Subject is nothing but its objects.

Therefore they are one—and *there is no "one."*

Perhaps that is all there is to be understood?

Subject must always be the absence of phenomenal presence: object (presence) must always be the presence of noumenal absence.

Intemporality must always be the absence of phenomenal time: temporality must always be the presence of the phenomenal absence of no-time.

But let us not forget, let us deeply comprehend that no word of this is the truth unless we have been profoundly penetrated by the understanding that there IS no subject and no object, no time and no no-time, no presence and no absence of anything.

The truth, as Shen Hui told us, is the noumenal absence of these phenomenal absences, as of these presences, their total conceptual absence, and, above all, the utter absence of such a thing as Truth itself, as of its absence.

For integral phenomenal and noumenal absence is the blinding radiance of the great white light which has been called Sat-Chit-Ananda, and which also is not at all—except as This-which-we-are.

II

As long as we are identified with an object: that is bondage.

As long as we think, act, live via an object, or as an object: that is bondage.

As long as we feel ourselves to be an object, or think we are such (and a "self" is an object): that is bondage.

That is what the Masters called the "guest" position, the "minister" position, the "functional" position.

When we know we are Subject only, when we live and act as Subject only, that is what the Masters called the "Host" position, the "Prince" position, "Principal" or "Potentiality."

All Else Is Bondage

All else is bondage.

All else must necessarily be bondage, for bondage is only THAT—and *that* is the illusory identification of Subject with its object.

Working on or through the phenomenal concept known as our "self" is working on or through the very false identification from which we are seeking to escape. Surely that is the way *in*, not the way *out?*

That is not the Masters' way; their rule, laid down by Hui Neng, was never to speak from the "guest," "minister," "functional" position, the position of the identified phenomenal object.

Their teaching was not a transmission of conceptual knowledge, but a process of persuasion and manœuver whereby the disciple was brought to perceive the way out of his identification by responding directly, and so assuming spontaneously the Master's own position of "Host," "Prince," "Principal."

Then he gently hit the Master, as the Master had hit him, or overturned the Master in his chair—and the Master laughed and was filled with joy, for he knew that his disciple was now aware of This-which-from-eternity-they-both-were.

21 · Ego

THE LATIN word *ego,* currently translated "I," in metaphysics implies subject, absolute subject, subject of every manifested object, physical or mental.

This ultimate subject has no attribute, quality or characteristic, other than that of not having any attribute, quality or characteristic, that is of never being any kind of object, for therein lies its pure subjectivity.

All manifestation is the object of subject, therefore all manifestation, all objectivisation, is nothing but subject, for there could not be anything else for any *thing* to be. Subject, then, is the potential of all that appears to be. But there is no such phenomenal thing as "subject" for, if there were, subject would thereby be an object, the object of the subject so conceiving it, and such a subject of subject would then be subject "itself" which cannot be conceived by "itself." Therefore subject can never be so named, can never be named or thought of at all. Nor could it ever in any circumstances be regarded, for it cannot see what it is not.

If we find it necessary to think or speak of it the best we can do is to use some term such as "potential," which may act as a symbol indicating what we seek to suggest. But, let us remember: *that* which thereby we seek to suggest can only be *this* which thereby is seeking to suggest, and this, be it "I" or "we," can never be known as a thing, as an object of thought, for THIS *has no objective existence* of any kind whatever.

All manifestation is nothing but THIS, which is here and now, and which is transcendent to motion, space and time, which are concepts which arise in sentient objects whereby they produce the appearance of the sensorially perceived universe. In the course of this process of manifestation absolute subjective potential becomes identified with each sentient being so manifested and such sentient beings then regard themselves as independent subjects possessing freedom of choice and action. This which pretends to choose and to act as a separate individual-being is subject in identification with its object, limited by objectivity, and is known as an "ego." This is the dualism of pseudo-subject and object, and is the cause of all the suffering that exists, or has ever existed, in the apparent universe.

That is why there is no such thing as an "ego," since it is only the illusory result of the identification of subject, which itself is the sentiency of sentient beings, with the apparent object that is sentient. As sentiency, the apparent being is pure subjective potentiality and nothing else whatever; as an object self-identified with its subject it is an ego-ridden monstrosity bound by concepts of good-and-evil, thinking by means of the comparison of opposing concepts. It is the cause of all known forms of suffering due to attempted exploitation, in its individual or group corporality, of its fellows and of all aspects of the sensorially-perceived universe by which its supposedly independent individual life is bounded.

Moreover every time a so-identified object thinks or acts as such, he is *objectifying his own subjectivity* and producing in himself that process known as *karma,* which is expressed in the suffering he inflicts and endures.

This is what bondage is, and liberation from bondage is the dissolution of this illusory limitation which is due to the identification of what he is as subject with an object, which *is* not as such, and which could never be a "self."

22 ·- Hommage à Hui Hai

IN THE first dialogue of his treatise Hui Hai asserts what amounts to the whole truth in one sentence.

He says, "Illumination means the realisation that Illumination is not something to be attained."

Illumination is not some thing—for it is not an object; nor is it "not to be attained" because we *possess* it already, as has inaccurately been stated—but because it is this-which-we-are.

As *that* for which we are searching, it is illusory, for it is in fact *this* "we" who are searching. This "we" who are searching cannot be found either, for we cannot find this-which-we-are by searching.

The realisation which "means" illumination, as Hui Hai puts it, is the result of discovering that the seeker, who is the sought, is nowhere to be found. Why is he not to be found? Because there is no such object as a seeker, nor anywhere for him to be. There is no object as such at all, never was, and never will be.

Hui Hai says it several times, in several ways: here he says it in answer to the first question posed, and in twelve simple words.

There is neither illumination nor absence of illumination, neither bondage nor liberation from bondage.

There is no one to be bound or freed. There is only one mind, which is not such at all as an object and which, therefore, having no subject could never incur any objective effect or condition of any kind whatever.

It is my phenomenal object, identified as "me," which thinks itself "bound" and seeks to be "freed," but it has never been bound and it will never be freed: *as soon as "I" no longer refers to "it"* (subject to its object) *there is no longer any "bondage" nor any "freedom," for such notions can no longer obtain.*

23 ⁓ The Answer to the Only Question

Practice? Who should be doing all that to whom?

You to yourself.

I have looked for myself for years, and have found no trace of anything but an object.

Why was that?

The question is the same—who is looking for what?

And the answer?

That which I was looking for was this which was looking.

So you found yourself after all?

Never.

How so?

There was no thing to be found. The sought was the searcher and the searcher was the sought; and nothing of the kind existed as an object.

And so?

That was the end of the search. There was nothing further to look for, nor need for any looking.

What then?

That is the answer to all questions.

All questions?

Absolutely all: the final answer to all questions. The complete answer.

I do not understand.

It cannot be understood. Understanding is the result of a process which uses mind objectively. Understanding is phenomenal, personal, and dead.

Then one should not try to understand?

Mind is noumenal, impersonal, subjective: that is why it is all that you are, all that anything is—and no thing itself.

I am just that?

No, you are neither that nor this. One just is, and doesn't know it. Everything just is, and doesn't know it. Such is what one finds when one wakes up. Asked the Awakened!

24 ·-- The Noumenal Answer

The chief hindrance is the identification with the body, the I-am-the-body idea?

Any identification with any object is an absolute hindrance, because "I" am totally devoid of objectivity, or of any trace-element thereof.

One can either seek to understand what one is, or what one is not?

I can only know what I am not. What I am is unknowable, for I am it, and if I could know it "I" would thereby be an object. Therefore *there is* no "it," and "I" am not.

You are, and you are not?

I neither am nor am not. There is no "I." If there were I would be an object. I am not at all, in any conceivable way, manner, state, form or dimension. For the same reason there is no such thing as Reality, Truth, Absolute, Self, Consciousness, Mind, Dharmakaya or any other concept whatever.

But there is I-am-not?

There is no I-am-not either. There is no thing, positive or negative, not even presence or absence. The Diamond Sutra, understood via Shen Hui's double negative, is the authority for that—if authority should be necessary, which it is not, for every sentient being is "I" and so can know this—for being and knowing are identical.

But there is no being or knowing!

There is no thing, nothing "been" or "known": all I can be or know is *such*—no thing.

What is Shen Hui's "double negative"?

In brief: absence of (the absence which is) the counterpart of presence, and absence of (the presence which is) the counterpart of absence. Or, if you prefer: absence of the concepts of absence of presence and of presence of absence.

Then what are objects?

Objects are I. The whole sensorially perceptible, knowable and imaginable universe is I.

So you are the universe?

Not at all: the universe is "I."

Pantheism maintains that God is the universe.

God is not the universe: the universe is God.

What is the difference?

In physics—none: in metaphysics—absolute difference, the difference between subject and object. The universe is not the subject of God.

Then the universe is both God and you?

Certainly not: it may be both God and "I."

So you are God?

Not at all: "God" is an object, your concept, and so are "you." As for me, this-which-I-am is not any thing at all.

Then nor is God?

Every concept is a *thing*, but, as such, is not. Neither "God" nor "I" is as an object.

You say that the universe is you. How do you know that?

I said that the universe is I. You can say it, every beetle, every sentient being can say it—*what* else is there that it could be, *where* else is there for it to be? Movement, space and time are only concepts. There can only be "I"—and I am not, no matter who says it.

Then why are the beetle, you and I different?

We are not different: we only appear to be different. Noumenally we are one: as phenomena (appearance), as one another's objects, we sensorially perceive and mentally interpret one another as the beetle, you and I. But as what we are, we *are not.*

So we are not—either phenomenally or noumenally?

Phenomenally we are not *as entities*, noumenally we are not as concepts—which also are objects. What we are is not entity or concept, objectivity of any kind, therefore we cannot either think or say that we are any thing—for that is what we are not.

Then can we not know ourselves at all?

We cannot "know" our selves at all, for we are not any thing to be known: we can only be ourselves—"our selves" being what-we-are.

And how is that to be done?

It is not to be done. It is. Everything is as it is.

Is there any authority for that?

Yes, indeed. But, as it is liable to be misunderstood, it has usually been implied rather than stated.

Then, regarding ourselves as some thing is the hindrance?

That alone is "bondage."

And the remedy?

To cease regarding the universe as an object (since it is I), objects as entities (since there are none), "yourself" and "others" as such (for neither ever was)! To look in the right direction, look up and look in, where there is no longer any direction at all—where no longer is there any *thing* to be measured from any *where* (nor any looking). Who then is there to be bound, to what then could there be any binding?

So that is Liberation?

Liberation for *whom?* From *what?* There has never been either.

And then you see that . . . ?

"It is as it is. That is all you can say," and they are Maharshi's words.

Which means that there is no entity or object at all as such, not even ourselves, not even "I"?

Not even "Not-I"! How could there be? Think, man, think! Does not thought unite with intuition in this ultimate insight? How . . . could . . . there . . . be?

Ha-ha-ha!

That is the answer, the answer which dualistic language cannot give, which can only be apperceived noumenally, that is by intuitive apprehension. Heartily I agree—Ha-ha-ha-ha!

But is laughter the correct reaction to this understanding?

Many have laughed, some have cried, a few have prayed. Bodhidharma told the Emperor that there was no doctrine and nothing holy about it, but the Emperor was too earnest a man even to understand.

And that is all it is?

One monk is reported as having said that, too. The phenomenal reaction is correct as laughter, but the final noumenal living of it is usually described as Bliss, and it expresses itself as Universal Benediction.

25 ⁓ Non-Entity

ONLY AN object can be "bound." Subject can neither be bound nor freed, hurt nor flattered, touched nor neglected.

"I" cannot possibly be an object, ever, anywhere, in any circumstances. *"I" can only be subject,* always, everywhere, in every circumstance. But, *as subject,* there is no "always"—for there is no time, there is no "where"—for there is no space, there are no "circumstances"—for there is no movement.

I am only eternal Subject—and neither in eternity nor in apparent time could I be known nor could there be anyone to know me—for no such entity as "I" could ever be.

II

I-subject cannot see, hear, feel, smell, taste or know, for only an object can have organs or attributes, and there is no one and no thing to be sensorially apprehended (see*ing*, hear*ing*, feel*ing*, tast*ing*, know*ing* are diversified phenomenal manifestations of the functional aspect, called *prajna,* of Absolute-I, which always "returns" to the immutable aspect, called *Dhyana,* which it has never left).

The apparent universe is a dream-structure in-formed by Subject, and therefore can be nothing but I-subject. For that reason nothing that happens therein can touch or reach the subject which it is. Both see-er and seen, hearer and heard, injurer and injured, are Subject, not as dualities but as unities. The man who hates me and hits me, and the me that is hated and hit, are both "I," not as two but as one. I who hate him and hit him in return, and he whom I hate and hit back, are both "I," for every possible phenomenal manifestation is in-formed by I-subject, and every possible phenomenal manifestation is objective whereas I am totally devoid of any element of objectivity.

Then I am pure Subjectivity? Indeed no: subjectivity is a state, some kind of conceptualised condition, if not an entity, and therefore an object. I am nothing of the kind, no thing of any kind whatever. "I" cannot be conceived or stated, supposed or suggested, indicated or known. As That I-am, I am not.

Yet there can never be a moment during which I can be anything but "I," nor you anything but "I," nor the beetle anything but "I." "I" am eternally awake, and "I," am a Non-entity.

Note:

Wu Wei and *Yu Wei*

THERE HAS NEVER BEEN A HEN WHO LAID AN EGG, but vast numbers of eggs have been laid by hens.

THERE HAS NEVER BEEN A MAN WHO WROTE A BOOK, but vast numbers of books have been written by men.

NO BODY HAS EVER DONE ANYTHING, but innumerable actions have been performed.

26 · Noumenal Living

BEING (or living noumenally, subjectively) is not ceasing to objectivise—for that is the functional aspect of subject—but ceasing to objectivise oneself, and thereby ceasing to regard one's objects as independent entities, as other than an aspect of oneself as their subject.

That, of course, implies that one is profoundly aware that one is not at all as any conceptual object, even a "being." That integral absence, both phenomenal and noumenal, is the necessary awareness of is-as-it-isness—commonly called Awakening.

27 · The Living Dream

The sought is the seeker,
The observed is the observer thereof,
That which is heard is the hearer of what is heard,
The odour is who inhales it,
The tasted is who savours what he tastes,
That which is touched is the feeler of it,
The thought is the thinker of the thought,
In brief, the sensorially perceived is the perceiver whose senses perceive.
And no perceiver of any sense-perception, or performer of any action, is to be found.

II

Let us take an example: you enter a restaurant, you *see* a table, you *hear* people talking, you *taste* what is on your plate, you *smell* the aroma of the wine in your glass, you *feel* the knife and fork in your hands, and you *know* that you are having lunch.

All this you sensorially perceive, and I have just pointed out to you that all this only took place in your mind, whose senses appeared to perceive it, and therefore that none of it actually happened as a series of external events experienced by you.

And finally I have stated that you yourself, as an independent entity whose senses appeared to experience these events, cannot be found anywhere. How can this be?

Let us recall the answer of the Sixth Patriarch Hui Neng to the monks who were arguing whether it was the flag or the wind that was flapping. He pointed out to them that it was their mind only which was responsible, and they recognised at once that he had understood the truth.

III

> There are no sentient beings to be delivered by the Tathagata. If even self has no objective existence how much less has other-than-self! Thus neither Buddha nor sentient beings exist objectively.
>
> —HUANG PO, Wan Ling Record 5, p. 70.

There is no such "thing" as a dream (or a mirage, an illusion, an hallucination), the dream as a thing-in-itself is not such. There is a phenomenon, an apparent dream-ing, just as there are ten thousand phenomena due to apparent see-ing, apparent hear-ing, feel-ing, smell-ing, tast-ing, apparent know-ing, but the objects apparently perceived by the senses are not entities at all. There is only a perceiv-ing of apparent objects mov-ing in apparent space in the apparent seriality of time.

In daily "life" the apparently "other" sentient beings who sensorially perceive the same phenomena that we perceive, synchronised in the same apparent time, are themselves also phenomena, mutually perceived or mutually not perceived, but there is nothing but the perceiv-ing, as in a dream there is nothing but the dream-ing. If the dreamer awakes the dream-ing ends, and there is no question regarding the "beings" or other phenomena in the dream, as to whether "they" are still pursuing their dream activities or are awake also. So in liv-ing, the awakened does not consider whether his fellows in the "living"-dream are now awake or are carrying on their "liv-ing"-dream, for he now knows that neither these nor that one of them which appeared to be himself was anything but a phenomenal object of the supposed dream-er. In both cases the apparent reality of the event dreamed has disappeared forever.

Where second-degree dreaming is concerned this is obvious to all of us, for we were the supposed dreamer and we are now awake, but in the first-degree or "living"-dream, which is essentially identical, we have difficulty in seeing it, for we are still participants in our dream and, as such, we are unaware that we are being dreamed.

However, in our first-degree or "living"-dream we have the possibility of becoming aware of this, and then each of us who does so can recognise that he is not the apparent entity in his particular dream that he believed himself to be, but the apparent dreamer of his own dream. That recognition too is called "Awakening." But he cannot then awaken the "others" in *his* late dream—for they were only his objects and were not entities in their own right any more than he was in the dream.

Therefore each dreamer can only awaken from his own dream, from the dream in which he himself participated as "himself," for even if his "liv-ing" friends appeared in his dream they did so only as his objects—which is as he happened to visualise them. "Others," therefore, are nothing but our objects; *as we know them* they are not entities in their own right, and they only *appear* to be such each as dreamer of his own dream, that is subjectively.

Awakened, however, each dreamer finds that he was the apparent subject of all the objects in his late dream of "living," but now is still not an entity—*for he no longer exists as an object except in the "living"-dream of "others."* He is the pure unconditioned subjectivity by means of which he was dreamed, as all other apparently sentient beings are dreamed, and whose apparent sentiency is nothing but that.

When the dreamed awakened from his sleeping-dream he was never the dreamer but was himself still being dreamed. There has never been a dream-er at all: there is just a phenomenon of dream-ing.

That, then, is what the "living"-dream is, i.e. an objectivisation in Mind in which the apparent entities are not such, and whose dreamer has never existed as an object and can never be an object in his own right—for there could never be any such "thing."

28 ·- Objets Perdus

Do you exist?

Noumenally I feel that I am, but I cannot find myself. And the same goes for you and for every living being.

Why is that?

For the same reason that prevents us from seeing our own face.

But you can see my face, and I can see yours.

Nonsense, perfect nonsense! We see nothing of the kind. What we see when we look at one another and at anything we can see at all, including our own feet, is just our object. And our object is part of ourself as its subject.

Nobody else can see us, because we have no objective existence whatever, and we cannot see anybody else because they have none. All of us can only see our own objectivisations—whatever they may be.

We do not exist as objects?

Of course not! No thing exists as an object. That is why there is no such thing as an entity. How could there be? Space and time are purely mental, concepts in mind. Where else could an entity extend itself?

Then no object is independent?

None is dependent either. "Other" are yourself as whatever you "both" are, and their apparent otherness as your objects is entirely a part of your phenomenal mind.

Phenomenal existence or being, noumenally is not being. Absolutely, it may be called as-it-isness.

I begin to understand!

Of course you do! "Is that all it is?," as the T'ang dynasty monk said, laughing, to his Master when he suddenly understood, or "found himself awake," as they put it.

II

No thing is—in its own right? Not even us?

No thing. Therefore there is no "us"—for "we" are only one another's objects as "us."

Then in what way are we?

Just total objective absence, which is the presence of that-I-amness, which is what-I-amness, which is this-I-amness.

All of us are that?

All of us are not "that," not "this," not any concept at all. Nothing mysterious about it. Nothing holy. Just phenomenal notness, and the absence of the concept of that (notness).

Then we have no positive being whatever?

Positivity and negativity are phenomenal concepts. We are not conceivable at all.

Then who lives?

You cannot find the doer of any deed, the thinker of any thought, the perceiver of any perception. The unfindable is all that we are, and the unfindable is the found.

> If you still cling to the notion that something, even if it be as small as the hundredth part of a grain, might exist objectively, then even a perfect mastery of the entire Mahayana canon will fail to give you victory over the Three Worlds. Only when every one of those tiny fragments is seen to be nothing can the Mahayana achieve this victory for you.
>
> —HUANG PO, Wan Ling Record 24, p. 86.

> There is no "self" and no "other." There is no "wrong desire," no "anger," no "hatred," no "love," no "victory," no "failure." Only renounce the error of conceptual thought processes and your nature will exhibit its pristine purity—for this alone is the way to attain enlightenment.
>
> —HUANG PO, Ibid. p. 88.

29 · Intentions

Only by avoiding intentions will the mind be rid of objects.

—SHEN HUI, h.5.

Only somebody who fancies that he lives according to his own good pleasure can have intentions. If he truly knows that as an apparent entity he is being *lived,* how can he harbour intentions?

He who knows that he is being lived must know that *as such* he cannot be the subject of objects. Since, being lived, he is no subject, objects cannot be his objects.

Therefore to know that one is being lived is to know what one is not, and to know what one is not is to know what one is.

II

Without "intentions" we do not have to form concepts; we just *act.* That alone is transcending conceptualisation. Not by suppressing concepts, if we could, but by abstaining from volition may we be in conformity with the requirements of the Masters.

Shen Hui tells us, "One without a purposeful intention is free from conceptualisation *(wu nien)."* Therefore it is the volitional activity of mind that is conceptual: nonvolitional activity of mind is *wu nien.*

But let us clearly understand that just as *wu nien* implies not only the absence of conceptualisation, but also the absence of its negative aspect, non-conceptualisation—that is absence also of volitional or conceptual not-thinking, so *wu wei* means not only the absence of volitional action (including the above) but also the absence of volitional non-action (of intentional or conscious or conceptual inactivity or not-doing).

III. Volition

The I-Notion alone can have "intentions"—for "ego" and "will" are synonymous. Therefore absence of the one is also absence of the other.

"Intentions" imply an act of will. The Taoist *wu wei* does not imply phenomenal inactions, but the absence of volitional action. The absence of volitional action implies the presence of noumenal action, which is the Taoist *Te*, the dynamic aspect of *Tao*. What, then, is noumenal action?

There is a positive implication in Shen Hui's definition of *wu nien* as a double absence, the absence of no-thought or of non-conceptualisation, which is the presence of that absence (see Chapter I), and that presence is the suchness of thought which is precisely spontaneous action. Non-volitional action (*wu wei*), whether perceptive, conceptive, or somatic is noumenal action, and noumenal action is the so-called "non-action" (non-volitional, non-egoitic action) of the Sage.

IV. Glad Living

> Just by avoiding purposeful intentions one can be enlightened.
>
> —SHEN HUI, h.5.

The attempt of a "lived" puppet to lead his own life is essentially the same as that of a "dreamed" puppet to lead his, and it is as real as any dream. Moreover these attempts are the only reality either could ever know.

But neither can "live." And neither is "lived" by an entity. Both are puppets reacting to impulses engendered by psychic conditions over which they have no control. Neither is sentient objectively, neither is an entity, the apparent sentiency of both is a reflex of the Mind which is all that they are.

The I-notion which has intention is itself such a reflex. Its performance as inaugurator of pretended acts of volition is a phantasy, and it is precisely this phantasy which constitutes suffering. In the absence of the phantasy of dreaming there is the bliss of deep sleep, and in the absence of the phantasy of living there is the bliss of "nirvana" or awakened life.

Intention is the temporal cause of psychological conflict, and purposeful intention is the temporal cause of physical conflict. Intemporally there is no intention, and without intention there is no counterpart to bliss, the term "bliss" being a conventional indication of the state of unconditioned being—which is devoid of any element of objectivity.

Volition, therefore, is the psychic chain which holds the phenomenal individual in apparent bondage, for volition is the pseudo-subject attempting to act independently of the force of circumstances. The absurdity of this performance should be sufficiently evident.

All the teaching of all the Masters of all the schools of liberation, not only Buddhic, Vedantic and Taoist, but Semitic also—as, witness, "Not my will but Thine, O Lord"—consists in attempts by means of knowledge, practices, and manreuvres to free the pseudo-individual from the chains of volition, for when that is abandoned no bondage remains.

The purest doctrines, such as those of Ramana Maharshi, Padma Sambhava, Huang Po and Shen Hui, just teach us that it is sufficient by analysis utterly to comprehend that there is no entity which could have effective volition, that an apparent act of volition when in accord with the inevitable can only be a vain gesture and, when in disaccord, the fluttering of a caged bird against the bars of his cage. When he knows that, then at last he has peace and is glad.

At a fair, when I was young, one could pretend to drive little motor-cars round and round a track. They had a steering-wheel which reacted to springs, but the vehicle was driven and steered automatically from below. Since one instinctively turned the wheel in the direction the little car had to go, it was difficult not to believe that one was steering it, and even more difficult to stop trying to steer it and leave it to take one where it would, for that might have been disaster. Such, *exactly,* is our volitional way of living.

Non-volitional living is glad living.

Being "lived," as a non-entity, is subjective living, in which suffering is no longer such, in which there is no place for care and for worry, in which everything is as-it-is and as it must be. For it is "intention" that is responsible for dualistic conception and the ensuing comparison of interdependent counterparts, seen as opposites, one of which is "good" and the other "bad."

Also it is noumenal living, and all that noumenal living is. It could also be termed Reintegration.

30 ·– *Non-Volitional Living*

ACADEMIC PSYCHOLOGY has long recognised that dreams are an expression of wish-fulfillment. It needs no science to tell us that day-dreams also are a factitious fulfillment of wishes. Both, therefore, are manifestations of an I-concept or "ego," of an identified pseudo-subject, of that which constitutes the egoity of the phenomenal individual.

Is not thinking of the future also a form of daydreaming, generally with a greater regard for probability? Is thinking of the past, either with pleasurable or with painful regret, intrinsically different from thinking of the future with hope or with fear? All are factitious wish-fulfillment positive or negative. All, therefore, are acts of volition.

That is why we are told by the Masters that nothing can be attained, that nothing is graspable, tangible, or can be possessed, and why we should ignore the future and ignore the past. That is also why past and future are said not to exist, for they are only suppositions, theoretical apparatus of dualistic living; both, as future and as past, are imagined and, since events are already passed by the time we have interpreted them, they have never existed otherwise than as events in consciousness. I think that has already been explained?

Past and future are just acts of volition. Therefore non-volitional living must be just living in the present. "Be present in the present," as Robert Linssen tells us. That is all that non-volitional living can be, but that does not mean that it exists as something that is happening. I have said above, and explained elsewhere, that everything we experience is the interpretation of a percept which is already passed in the conditioned reflex which we know as time. Presence in the now-moment is eternal: it is intemporal. Phenomenally we cannot know it. Robert Linssen's "present au present" is, phenomenally, non-volitional living but, noumenally, is finding ourselves in the intemporality of awakened being—which is our eternal heritage.

Tao, the pathless Way, has a gateless Gate which, just as the Equator separates the Northern from the Southern hemisphere, illusorily separates and unites the phenomenal and the noumenal, *samsara* and *nirvana.* It is the open road of escape from solitary confinement in the dungeon of individuality. It is the way of reintegration in this-which-we-are, and it is pure as-it-isness.

31 ⁓ *Ultimate Illusion*

The Illusion of Voluntary Action

The phenomenal object must be entirely conditioned (subject to cause-and-effect).

The phenomenal subject is entirely illusory.

The Unconditioned can have no attribute (such as Will).

In Temporality (subject to the time-concept) Volition is an appearance (phenomenon), like every other appearance, an apparent element of the mechanism of living. It has no self-nature (is not as such): its only existence is its phenomenal absence.

An apparent entity is "lived" or "dreamed": his is a role played by an "actor." The *dramatis persona* has no volition at his disposal: the apparent volition displayed is a pretence inherent in the part; and the energy via which that part is played is not subject to a volitional act.

For the "actor" is not an entity, but Mind-Only.

Note: The Buddha's teaching, much emphasised by the Masters, that there is nothing to attain (obtain, grasp, reach, etc.) is significant, for these are all terms for an act of volition.

Not only can so-called Englightenment not be "attained" by anybody, as it was not "attained" by the Buddha, but *there is no Volitional attainment* whatever.

32 · Tao

The Doctrine is the doctrine of non-doctrine,
The Practice is the practice of non-practice,
The Method is meditation by non-meditation,
And Cultivation which is cultivation by non-cultivation.

This is the Mind of non-mind, which is *wu hsin,*
The Thought of non-thought, which is *wu nien,*
The Action of non-action, which is *wu wei,*
The Presence of the absence of Volition,
Which is Tao.

33 · Elimination of Bondage

CAUSE-AND-EFFECT ARE temporal manifestations: intemporally they are one. Temporally, volition is a causal factor (an immediate cause), itself an effect.

When the informing Mind (the unnameable—because non-objective—factor which informs all appearance) shines through the mist which results from identification with a phenomenal object, volition becomes illusory, since it is of the texture of that mist.

Cause-and-effect continue to operate, but volition as a causal factor is eliminated. A body is still lived by causation, but the phenomenal aspect of mind, the split (dualistic) aspect of subject-and-object, is freed from all that depended on volition, affective or intellectual, and is thereby liberated.

34 ·- *Personally to You*

IF ONE has understood this, profoundly understood it, is there any longer a reason why one should go on living in subjection to an identification with a psycho-somatic "I" which one now clearly knows is not what one is? Has one not realised that a "self" is only one's object, perceptual and conceptual, and that it could not be what we are?

If so, one is free to snap out of that fixation and to live as one is—for one "is as one is," and one must always be that, from whatever illusory notions one may suffer. Can one not just "live free"—like Elsa the lioness—without abandoning one's "lifelong" associations, the "state of life to which it has pleased God to call us," though now without affective attachment? Can one not go on playing one's part in the play of everyday life, as the actor does in his, liv-ing out one's liv-ing dream, simply and worthily, though without remaining identified with it or "without taking it seriously" as one says? Envy, hatred and malice will be no more, vengeance will no longer seem desirable, we shall be invulnerable, and we know why—for we have said it again and again in the foregoing pages—and so there is no one to hurt any "us." Love and hatred are replaced by universal benediction, manifested as kindliness and good nature towards the world around us which we now recognise as ourself.

We may regard this simply as living noumenally instead of phenomenally, though it may be that pure noumenal living represents a further degree of insight, such as that in which Maharshi and the great sages lived out their "lives." But degrees are conceptual, and every liv-ing thing is only Buddha-mind (which is all a Buddha is) whatever his degree of attachment, and recognising "degrees" is living phenomenally.

The Sages did not consistently conform to any pattern of saintliness, their phenomenal manifestations were on occasion quite ungodly. Their phenomenality was not confined to their corporeal functions. Sai Baba was often violent, though such manifestations were momentary and rootless, perhaps deliberate. Our notions concerning the behaviour of Sages are only concepts; and anyhow they are not to be copied. We have only to live noumenally—and that implies an awareness which is not aware of itself and which has no room for conceptuality.

Let us do this. Let us live gladly! Quite certainly we are free to do it. Perhaps it is our only freedom, but ours it is, and it is only phenomenally a freedom. "Living free" is being "as one is." Can we not do it now? Indeed can we not-do-it? It is not even a "doing": it is beyond doing and not-doing. It is being as-we-are.

This is the only "practice."

Other Spiritual Classics by Wei Wu Wei

Open Secret

In poetry, dialogs, epigrams, and essays, Wei Wu Wei addresses our illusions concerning the mind, the self, logic, time, space, and causation, and gives a substantive interpretation of *The Heart Sutra.*

ISBN 81-8328-013-7

The Tenth Man, Foreword by Dr. Gregory Tucker

In giving us his version of the perennial philosophy, Wei Wu Wei brings a very different perspective to the conventional notions about time, love, thought, language, and reincarnation.

ISBN 81-86685-64-2

Posthumous Pieces, Foreword by Wayne Liquorman

This work was not published after the author's death. Rather, these profound essays and epigrams are "tombstones, a record of living intuitions."

ISBN 81-8328-012-9

Unworldly Wise

Wu Wei's final book is an enlightened parable in the form of a conversation between a wise owl and a naïve rabbit about God, friendship, loneliness, and religion.

ISBN 978-81-8328-128-7